P9-DEY-263

On cold nights, plants may get so cold that moisture in the air freezes onto them instantly, instead of forming liquid dew. This is called hoar frost.

Lightning flashes between the bottom of the thundercloud and the ground.

Sun

Igloos are dome-shaped houses built of solid blocks of snow.

"Wet" snow makes good snowballs.

Weather

Written by John Farndon

Consultant: John Woodward

Senior editor Gill Pitts
Editor Olivia Stanford
Assistant editor Kritika Gupta
Editorial assistance Cécile Landau
US Senior editor Margaret Parrish
Senior art editor Ann Cannings
Project art editor Yamini Panwar
Illustrators Abby Cook, Dan Crisp, Shahid Mahmood
Jacket co-ordinator Francesca Young
Jacket designers Dheeraj Arora, Amy Keast, Faith Nelson
DTP designers Dheeraj Singh, Jagtar Singh

Picture researcher Aditya Katyal
Producer, pre-production Nadine King
Producer Isabell Schart
Managing editors Soma B. Chowdhury,
Laura Gilbert, Monica Saigal
Managing art editors Neha Ahuja Chowdhry,
Diane Peyton Jones
Art director Martin Wilson
Publisher Sarah Larter
Publishing director Sophie Mitchell

Original edition
Project editor Christine Webb
Art editors Thomas Keenes, Carol Orbel
Senior editor Susan McKeever
Senior art editor Jacquie Gulliver
Production Catherine Semark
Editorial consultant Ron Lobeck
Illustrators John Bendall-Brunello, Julia Cobbold,
Louis Mackay, Richard Ward

First American Edition, 1992
This edition published in the United States in 2017 by
DK Publishing, 345 Hudson Street, New York, New York 10014

Copyright © 1992, 1998, 2017 Dorling Kindersley Limited
DK, a Division of Penguin Random House LLC
17 18 19 20 21 10 9 8 7 6 5 4 3 2
004–298511–Apr/2017

A catalog record for this book is available from the Library of Congress.
ISBN 978-1-4654-5755-4

DK books are available at special discounts when purchased in bulk for sales promotions, premiums, fund-raising, or educational use.
For details, contact: DK Publishing SpecialMarkets, 345 Hudson Street, New York, New York 10014 SpecialSales@dk.com

Printed and bound in China

The publisher would like to thank the following for their kind permission to reproduce their photographs:
(Key: a-above; b-below/bottom; c-center; f-far; l-left; r-right; t-top)
4 123RF.com: Derrick Neill (tl); Taina Sohlman (cra). **Alamy Stock Photo:** Design Pics Inc (bl). **Dreamstime.com:** Dmytro Kozlov (b).
9 NASA: (cr). **10 123RF.com:** Andrew Mayovskyy (crb). **Ann Cannings:** (cr). **Dreamstime.com:** Konart (bc). **11 123RF.com:** PaylessImages (cl). **Dreamstime.com:**
Marsia16 (clb). **16 123RF.com:** andersonrise (cr); oasis15 (t, br). **18 Dreamstime.com:** Sabine Katzenberger (bl). **Rex by Shutterstock:** Amos Chapple (cr). **19 123RF.
com:** (t). **20-21 123RF.com:** mrtwister (b). **22 123RF.com:** Thomas Fikar (b). **23 123RF.com:** Wasin Pummarin (t). **Getty Images:** Keystone (b). **24 123RF.com:** alexse
(cr); Taina Sohlman (bl). **Dreamstime.com:** Furtseff (tl). **25 123RF.com:** PaylessImages (t). **Alamy Stock Photo:** Andrew Rubtsov (crb). **26 Fotolia:** Alexandr Ozerov
(cl). **27 Alamy Stock Photo:** Design Pics Inc (b). **Dreamstime.com:** Dmytro Kozlov (bl/Snowballs); Yael Weiss (cr). **29 123RF.com:** jezper (br). **30 iStockphoto.com:**
Artur Synenko. **32 123RF.com:** Meghan Pusey Diaz / playalife2006 (b). **Corbis:** Warren Faidley (cr). **34 123RF.com:** Anton Yankovyi (cl). **34-35 Dreamstime.com:**
Justin Hobson. **35 123RF.com:** Darko Komorski (cla); sebastien decoret (crb). **36 123RF.com:** smileus (br). **Alamy Stock Photo:** imageBROKER (cra). **39 Corbis:**
Bettmann (cr). **41 Dreamstime.com:** Nuralya (tr). **46-47 123RF.com:** Derrick Neill. **47 123RF.com:** Pornkamol Sirimongkolpanich (r). **48 Alamy Stock Photo:** United
Archives GmbH (cl). **49 123RF.com:** manachai Phongruchirapha (tl). **51 123RF.com:** Pablo Hidalgo (t). **Alamy Stock Photo:** Morley Read (b). **52 123RF.com:** Nikole
Grigoriev (t). **iStockphoto.com:** Heiko Küverling (bl). **54 123RF.com:** oceanfishing (cra). **PunchStock:** Design Pics (clb)

Cover images: Front: **Dreamstime.com:** Furtseff (tl), Motorolka (cr); **Getty Images:** DAJ (tc), MyLoupe (bl); Back: **Alamy Stock Photo:** Design Pics Inc
(bl); **Dreamstime.com:** Gsk2013 (cl); **iStockphoto.com:** Artur Synenko (tr); Spine: **Dreamstime.com:** Motorolka t/ (Maple Leaf)

All other images © Dorling Kindersley
For further information see: www.dkimages.com

A WORLD OF IDEAS:
SEE ALL THERE IS TO KNOW
www.dk.com

Contents

What is weather?

Weather is just the way the air around you changes all the time. It can be still, moving, hot, cold, wet, or dry. Most importantly, weather is the way water changes in the air. Without water, there would be no clouds, rain, snow, thunder, or fog. The weather plays a big part in our lives and affects many of the things that we do.

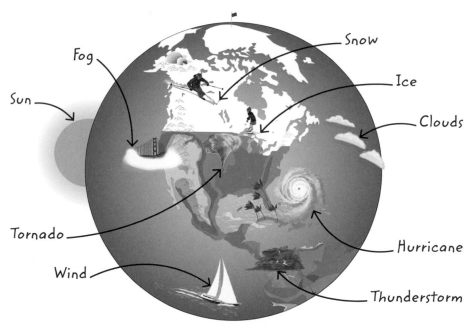

Snow

Ice

Clouds

Fog

Sun

Tornado

Wind

Hurricane

Thunderstorm

Weather places

Weather is different in different parts of the world. In deserts, for instance, it very rarely rains, while in tropical jungles, it is hot and steamy. Climate is the usual kind of weather that a place has over a long period. For example, the Arctic has a cold climate.

The atmosphere

Our planet is surrounded by a thin blanket of gases called the atmosphere. Weather only happens in the very lowest layer, the troposphere.

Satellites are stationed in the exosphere, 600 to 300 miles (1,000 to 500 km) from Earth.

The thermosphere is between 300 and 55 miles (500 and 85 km) from Earth. Here, you'll find the aurora lights and the International Space Station.

The mesosphere is between 55 and 30 miles (85 and 50 km) from Earth. Some of the ozone layer and meteorites are found here.

Weather forecasts

Weather experts use satellites to help them make more accurate forecasts. This satellite photograph shows a hurricane over an ocean.

The stratosphere is between 30 and 7 miles (50 and 12 km) from Earth. Nacreous clouds sometimes appear in the lower level, and passenger planes often fly this high.

All our weather happens in the troposphere.

The ancient Greeks used to think that wind was the Earth breathing in and out. Now we know it is simply air on the move.

The seasons

You can expect a certain kind of weather at certain times of the year. Winter days are often bitterly cold or stormy, while summer days may be warm and sunny. It all depends on the season. Some places have just two seasons, a wet one and a dry one. Other places have four: spring, summer, fall, and winter.

Spring
Once winter is over, the Sun climbs higher in the sky, and the days get longer. Nights are cold but days can be warm.

Winter
Winter is the coldest time of year. The days are so short and the Sun hangs so low in the sky that the air barely warms up.

Hot Christmas
Because of the way the seasons work, winter happens in the United States when it is summer on the opposite side of the world, in Australia.

Cold winters bring snow.

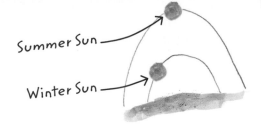

Flowers grow in summer sunshine.

High and low

The seasons occur because the amount of sunlight reaching you varies. In summer, you will see that the Sun is much higher than in winter. This means that your part of the Earth is tilting toward the Sun.

Summer

The Sun is high in the sky at noon, and days are long and warm. Hot weather may be broken by thunderstorms.

Fall

During fall, the nights get longer and cooler again. Mornings are often misty. Sometimes they are frosty.

Fall usually brings mists.

Winter sleep

Many animals, such as dormice, sleep away the winter to save energy. This is called hibernation.

The three clouds

Clouds come in all kinds of shapes and sizes, but they are all made of billions of tiny water droplets or even ice crystals floating in the sky. There are three basic types—wispy "cirrus" clouds, fluffy white "cumulus" clouds, and huge blankets of "stratus" clouds.

Cirrus clouds

Feathery cirrus clouds form very high up in the sky. It is so cold up there that they are made not of water droplets, but of tiny ice crystals.

Cirrus clouds high up in the sky often signal bad weather.

Mare's tails

Cirrus clouds are often called mare's tails, because strong winds high in the air blow them into wispy curls—just like the tail of a horse.

What makes a fluffy cloud?

Cumulus clouds form when sunshine warms up bubbles of moist air and causes them to rise quickly. As they get higher, they swell and are cooled so that the moisture turns into a mist of water droplets.

This cloud's fluffy shape shows how the bubble of warm, moist air billows out.

Cumulus clouds

Fluffy cumulus clouds are the clouds you usually see in clear weather, when the sky is blue. They look like heaps of cotton balls and are always changing shape. They are about 1,650 ft (500 m) above you.

Stratus clouds build up when warm, moist air rides up slowly over a bank of colder air.

Stratus clouds

The word "stratus" means "layers" in Latin, but you rarely see the layers in a stratus cloud. You just see a huge gray sheet of low cloud that can stretch for hundreds of miles.

Cloudspotting

Clouds come in many shapes and sizes—some large and fluffy, some small and wispy. It all depends on whether they are formed from water droplets or ice crystals. Weather experts identify clouds by how high they are in the sky, and whether they are layered (stratus) or in heaps (cumulus).

Cirrostratus

Clouds that form very high in the sky always start with the word "cirro." Cirrostratus clouds are made of ice crystals.

Altostratus

Medium-height clouds start with the word "alto." Altostratus is a layer of cloud made of water droplets.

Nimbostratus

These thick layers of cloud start near the ground and can be very tall. They can bring hours of rain or snow.

Stratus

Thick layers of stratus cloud hang close to the ground. Sometimes the Sun can be seen through them, looking like a silver disk.

Cirrocumulus

These tiny balls of icy cloud often form what is called a "mackerel sky," because they look like the scales of a mackerel fish.

Cirrus

Cirrus tend to be the highest clouds of all. They form streaks across the sky that tell of strong winds blowing. They are a sign of unsettled weather.

Altocumulus

These are medium-height cumulus clouds. They look like flattened balls of cotton that are almost joined together.

Cumulus

Fluffy cumulus clouds are easy to spot. These low-level clouds sometimes develop during the day and get bigger, giving showers.

Cumulonimbus

These are the towering clouds that give us thunderstorms and even tornadoes. A big one may be taller than Mount Everest!

Stratocumulus

If you see long rolls of these medium-height clouds, this usually means fair weather is on the way. They are made by cumulus clouds spreading out in layers.

Wet air

You might not know it, but you're sitting in a sea of water. Like a sponge, air soaks up invisible water vapor. All air contains water vapor, but how much it holds—the air's "humidity"—depends on how hot and dry it is where you are.

Wet breath

When you breathe out, you fill the air with water vapor. If the air is very cold, the vapor turns into millions of tiny water droplets and your breath looks "steamy."

Dew wonder

If air cools down, it can hold less water. After a cool night, leaves and grass are often covered in drops of water, or dew, that the air could not hold.

Dew drops

THE WATER CYCLE

Rain is the same water going around and around in a never-ending circle called the water cycle.

High up, water vapor turns into drops of water. This is called "condensation."

Big clouds are so full of water that some falls to the ground as rain.

Some rainwater seeps through the ground before reaching rivers.

1. Damp air
Water gets into the air because the Sun heats up oceans and lakes. Millions of gallons of water then rise into the air as invisible water vapor. This is called "evaporation."

2. Falling rain
When some clouds get big, the droplets of water in them bump into each other and grow. They get so big that they fall to the ground as rain. This is called "precipitation."

3. Running away
Some rain falls straight into the sea. Rain falling on the ground fills up rivers and streams, which run back to the sea, then the cycle begins all over again.

Rain and drizzle

Without clouds, it wouldn't rain. Rain is simply water falling from clouds of tiny water droplets. Clouds form because air currents carry air up until it cools, and the water vapor turns into drops of water, which fall as rain. When the raindrops are very fine, they fall as drizzle.

Record rainfall

The wettest place in the world is Mawsynram village in India, where up to 467 in (11,872 mm) of rain falls every year.

Raining ice

Sometimes rain falls as solid chunks of ice, called hailstones. These are made when raindrops are tossed high up in huge clouds, and freeze into ice. As they are bounced up and down inside the cloud, they grow into big hailstones.

See how the ice builds up in layers, like the layers of an onion.

Base of large gray thundercloud, full of water

Rain approaching

This picture shows a heavy rainstorm over the Grand Canyon in the United States. Short, heavy showers like this are common in warm places, because the warmth can make air rise rapidly to create big rainclouds.

Weather clue

According to some country folk, you know rain is on its way when cows are all lying down in a field. Unfortunately, the cows sometimes get it wrong!

Raindrops

Every cloud holds millions of water droplets and ice crystals. They are so tiny that they are held up by air alone. Some big clouds have water droplets at the bottom and ice crystals at the top. Before rain falls, the droplets grow much bigger. Some grow by bumping into one another and joining together. Others grow by condensation.

See how they grow

In clouds forming high in the sky, water vapor freezes onto ice crystals, and they grow into snowflakes. Then they fall from the cloud. As they fall through warmer air, they melt into raindrops.

Tiny water droplets bump into each other and cling together as they fall.

Drop by drop

As a raindrop falls, it gathers up smaller ones below, growing all the time. The biggest raindrops are about 1/5 in (5 mm) across. But drizzle measures less than 0.02 in (0.5 mm) across.

Raindrops send up a splash of water. However, drizzle does not make splashes on water.

MAKE A RAIN GAUGE

If you want to keep a record of how much rain falls, you can make yourself a simple rain gauge like this. You will need a large plastic soft-drink bottle, scissors, tape, a measuring cup, a heavy flower pot, a notepad, and a pencil.

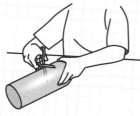

1. With an adult present, use a pair of scissors to cut the neck off the bottle. Set the neck to one side, but don't throw it away!

2. Use the measuring cup to pour $1/2$ cup (100 ml) of water into the bottle. Mark the level with tape and then pour in more water, marking each $1/2$ cup (100 ml) until it is full.

4. Set your gauge outside in a heavy flowerpot (to stop it from blowing over). Every day, or week, if you prefer, make a note of how much water there is in the bottle, using the marks to help you.

3. Empty the water out and attach the neck of the bottle upside down to the bottom with tape.

Every time you measure the water, you can plot the result on a graph.

21

Fog and mist

On a clear day, you can see for miles if you are high enough. But at other times the air may be so thick with fog that you can barely see across the road. Fog and mist look like smoke, but they are just tiny drops of water floating in the air. In fact, they are clouds that have formed at ground level.

Morning mist

Mist is made in the same way as fog, but is not as thick as fog. It clings close to the ground, and you can see over the top of it. Long, clear fall nights often bring misty mornings—especially in valleys, because cold air drains down into a valley during the night.

Mist is thickest just above the ground, because it is the ground that cools the air.

Golden mist

San Francisco's Golden Gate Bridge is often wrapped in mist because the warm California air is chilled by cold ocean currents.

Night fog

It gets foggy when the air is too cool to hold all its moisture, or water vapor. At night when the sky is clear, the ground gets cold. It cools the air close to it, making water droplets form in the air. The thickest fogs form when the air holds a lot of moisture.

Fog cuts visibility (the distance you can see) to less than 3,300 ft (1,000 m).

Souper fog

Dust and smoke make fog much worse. Before coal fires were banned in London in the 1950s, the city had some of the world's worst fogs, called "pea-soupers" because they were so thick and yellow-green!

23

Frost and ice

In winter, the days are short and the Sun hangs low in the sky, so we barely feel its warming rays. On clear nights, there is no blanket of clouds to keep in even this warmth. In some countries, it gets so cold that moisture in the air freezes, covering the ground with sparkling frost.

Pretty cold!

If you live in a country where it gets very cold, you may see lovely patterns of fern frost on your windows. This is made when tiny water drops on the glass turn into ice. As more moisture freezes on top of these icy drops, feathery fingers of frost begin to grow.

When moisture in the air freezes, it becomes frost.

Frosty nights

On cold nights, plants may get so cold that moisture in the air freezes onto them instantly, instead of forming liquid dew. This is called hoar frost.

Rime frost only
forms on one side.

Ice needles

If fog forms in very cold air, the tiny
water droplets that make up the fog
freeze onto anything they touch.
The ice builds up in thick layers
called rime. This is often swept
into strange shapes by the wind.

Winter fun

It is lucky for us that ice floats
on water. When it is really
cold, ponds, lakes, and canals
are covered with a layer of
ice. If ice sank, not only lakes
but all the seas would slowly
turn into solid ice!

Ice is frozen water.

 Never walk or skate on ice unless an
adult has first checked that it is safe!

Snowy weather

High up where the air is below freezing, clouds are made up of tiny ice crystals. These crystals grow into large snowflakes, which drift downward and melt if the air gets warmer nearer the ground. However, if it is near or below freezing all the way down to the ground, we get snow instead.

White blanket

Once snow has covered the ground, it may not melt for a while, because the white snow reflects warming sunlight. If it melts and then refreezes, the crisp blanket will last even longer.

It snows the most when the temperature is at freezing point, which is 32°F (0°C).

Winter sports

Snowy weather can have its benefits! Skiing and sledding down a snow-covered slope are popular winter sports.

SNOW WONDER

Put some snowflakes on a colored surface and look carefully at them under a magnifying glass. You will see that they all have a six-pointed shape. However, just as no two people are exactly the same, no two snowflakes are identical.

You'll have to work quickly before they melt!

Actual size of a snowflake.
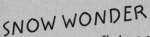

Snowflakes look like delicate lace.

All sorts of snow

When it is below freezing, snow is powdery and "dry" and is useless for making snowballs. However, when the temperature is just about freezing, the snow is "wet" and easily crushed into heavy snowballs.

Igloos are dome-shaped houses built of solid blocks of snow.

"Wet" snow makes good snowballs.

From breeze to gale

Winds are simply the air around us moving. Sometimes the air moves so slowly that the wind is too weak to lift a feather. At other times, it moves so fast that trees and walls are blown down. Strong winds can be very dangerous. The Beaufort wind scale divides winds into 13 "forces." On the Beaufort wind scale, 0 is calm and 12 is a hurricane.

Clouds sweep across the sky

Force 2: Light breeze
When a light breeze blows, the weather is usually clear. You can feel air on your face, hear leaves rustle, and see plumes of smoke gently drifting.

Force 5: Fresh breeze
During a fresh breeze, clouds often start to drift across the sky, and small trees sway. Crested waves form on lakes.

Force 7: Near gale
During a near gale, the sky may be dark and stormy. Large trees sway and it becomes hard to walk against the wind.

Force 9: Strong gale
When the wind blows at strong gale force, the sky may be covered in thick cloud. Large branches snap and chimneys and roof tiles can be blown off.

Wind power
Windmills were once used to grind grain. Now they are used to make electricity. Forests of windmills like these can make enough electricity to light a whole town.

Under pressure

You can't feel it, but the air is pushing down on you all the time. This push is called air pressure. Sometimes pressure is high; sometimes it is low. Changes in air pressure bring changes in the weather and make winds blow.

Ups and downs

Changes in air pressure are measured on an instrument called a barometer. When pressure is low, the weather is often wet and cloudy. When it is high, the weather is usually dry and clear.

When the air pressure drops, stormy weather is on the way.

This barometer measures pressure in units called hectopascals (hPa), which are the equivalent of millibars (mb).

When air pressure stays high, the weather is likely to stay clear.

MAKE A BAROMETER

This barometer will help you predict the weather. Make it on a rainy day when the air pressure is low, or it will not work. You will need a jam jar or straight-sided glass, a long-necked bottle, water mixed with food coloring, and a marker.

1. Set the bottle upside down in the jar so that it rests on the rim. The top of the bottle should not quite touch the bottom of the jar.

2. Take the bottle out and pour enough colored water into the jar so that it just covers the neck of the bottle when it is in place. On the jar, mark the level of the water in the bottle.

3. Set your barometer in a place where the temperature is fairly constant. Mark any changes in the water level over the next few weeks.

When the water is high in the bottle, pressure is high and it should stay clear.

When the water is low in the bottle, pressure is low and you can expect storms.

Right windy

Because the world is spinning, winds spin, too—out of high and into low-pressure areas. Try standing with your back to the wind. If you live north of the equator, high pressure will be on your right. South of the equator, it will be on your left.

Superwinds

In summer, tropical places are hot and sunny. During the fall, the skies darken and storms sweep in from the sea, bringing fierce winds and lashing rain. These storms are called hurricanes, typhoons, or tropical cyclones, depending on where you live.

Tropical revolving storm

A hurricane starts when hot tropical sunshine stirs up moist air over the sea. It then whirls over the ocean in a giant spinning wheel of cloud, wind, and rain.

Picture of a hurricane taken from a satellite in space

Blown away

Howling hurricane winds can do terrible damage. On the coast, huge waves raised by the winds can swamp the shore.

Hurricane slice

What goes on inside a hurricane? Fierce winds hurtle around the bottom of the storm, but the center is dead calm. The air that spirals up around the center builds up tall rain clouds.

Warm, damp air spirals up around the center of the storm, making huge clouds.

Hurricanes may be 900 miles (1,500 km) across and 7 miles (12 km) or more high. Hurricane winds in the Northern Hemisphere spin in the opposite direction of the hurricane winds in the Southern Hemisphere.

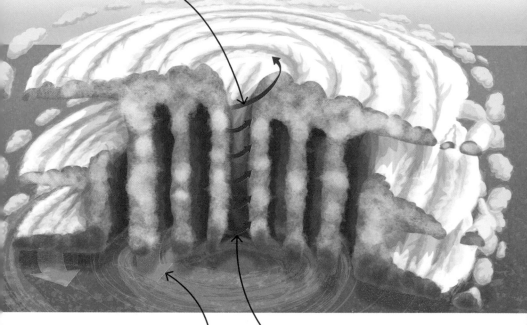

Hurricane winds blow around the base of the storm at 185 mph (300 kph) or more.

The air in the very center, or "eye," of the storm is clear and calm.

Every hurricane is given a name. Once, only girls' names such as Jane and Diana were used, but now boys' names are used, too.

Twisters

Twisters, or tornadoes, are whirling funnels of
air. They hang down from thunderstorm clouds,
which form in very hot and humid weather.
Twisters usually last about 15 minutes, but if
the bottom of a funnel touches the ground,
it will smash everything in its path instantly.

Twisters are
like the funnel
that forms
when water
is sucked
down a
drain.

Twister alert

If you see thunderclouds with small,
rounded "lumps" beneath them,
they are a good sign that a tornado
is on the way. These bulging clouds
are called mammatus clouds.

White column

Inside a tornado, air is sucked upward and
starts to spin at enormous speed. An approaching
tornado is white, because it has not yet touched
the ground and picked up dust and debris.

Waterspout

When a tornado develops over calm seas, it is called a waterspout. Mist, spray, and water are sucked up into the twisting funnel.

Tornadoes are most common in the United States.

On target

A tornado makes a deafening roar as it passes by. As the bottom of a tornado touches the ground, it sucks dust and debris high into the sky. It can also lift heavy objects before hurling them back to the ground.

At the center of a tornado, wind speeds can reach 250 mph (400 kph). They are the fastest winds on Earth.

Hot weather

In places where the Sun sits high in the sky at noon, the days are long and the weather is hot. Hot weather often comes with high pressure areas, because they bring clear skies and light winds. High pressure can last for a long time, making hot, sunny weather last for days on end.

Mirage

Sometimes, on a very hot day, you may see a mirage—a pool of water on the road ahead. Then, as you approach, it disappears. What you are actually seeing is the reflection of the sky on a layer of hot air just above the ground.

Thermometer

Thermometers help us to measure the temperature. Sealed inside a glass tube is some dyed alcohol. The liquid expands as the temperature rises and shrinks as it gets colder.

Glass tube holding alcohol dyed blue.

THE POWER OF THE SUN

The Sun gives off energy, which we feel as heat. Its energy can be trapped by solar panels and made into electricity.

If the day starts sunny with few clouds, the temperature soon starts to rise.

The Sun is high in the sky.

Short trails of condensation are left by the aircraft.

"Heat-haze" is made when dust and pollution are trapped near ground level.

A hot, dry day

On a hot day, if the air is dry and calm, there are no clouds in the sky. Hot, humid weather is more unpleasant, because water vapor in the air makes us feel sticky and uncomfortable.

Dry weather

Some countries have plenty of water and shortages are rare. However, in some parts of the world water is scarce, and people can never be sure when it will rain next. Droughts happen when for months—or even years—on end, the Earth's surface loses more water than it collects. In some places, called deserts, rain hardly ever falls at all.

Drought

If droughts last for a very long time, animals die of thirst, crops wither in the hot Sun, and people have to go without food—they may even die of starvation.

Parched, cracked land

In true deserts, plants and animals can only live near oases, which are areas of open water.

Desert scene

You'll often find deserts inland, next to mountain ranges. The mountains act as a shield and keep rain-bearing clouds away. Semideserts like this one in Arizona, in the United States, have a little rainfall—enough to support plants that can store water, like cacti.

Death Valley

One of the driest and hottest places in the world is Death Valley, in the United States. People have died of thirst here in the extreme heat.

Not all deserts are hot. Central Antarctica is one of the driest places on Earth.

Dust Bowl

Drought can affect many people's lives. In the 1930s, The Great Plains of North America suffered from a disastrous drought that created a "dust bowl." Terrible dust storms buried crops and houses, and many people were forced to leave their homes.

Large stones at corners

Small pebbles to weigh down center

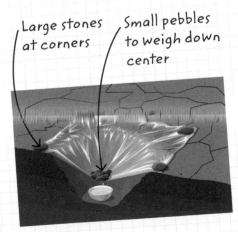

MAKE A GARDEN MOISTURE TRAP

Dig a hole and put a bowl in the center. Cover it with plastic, held down by stones. The next day, you'll see water in the bowl. This happens because water evaporates from the soil and condenses on the plastic, running off into the bowl.

Monsoon

A monsoon is a seasonal wind that blows for about six months in one direction, then turns around and blows in the other direction for six months. In summer, moist winds from the ocean bring dark, rain-bearing clouds to the land. In winter, the cycle is reversed. Wind blows the air from the land to the sea, bringing cool, dry weather.

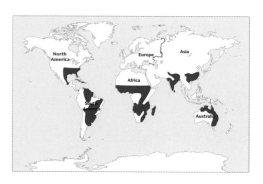

The monsoon areas are colored red.

Where the wind blows

The monsoon is best known in Asia, but monsoon winds also bring rain to other places in the tropics including Africa, South America, the southern United States, and Australia.

Before the monsoon

During the early summer, the hot Sun heats up the dry tropical land, while the seas and oceans stay cooler. As warm air rises above the land, cool, moist air from the sea rushes in to fill its place. The winds blowing the sea air bring heavy rainfall.

Life goes on

The rain is often so heavy that it washes away crops and floods the streets. Violent thunderstorms can also occur, but whatever the monsoon brings, life goes on.

Monsoon in action

Monsoons are vital for growing crops. Once the monsoon begins, the wet conditions are ideal for rice farmers, who can start planting young rice plants in the flooded fields.

After the rain

For six months, showers sweep across the land. Finally, the wind and rain die down. The cool air flows back toward the sea and the land begins to dry.

A warm front

If weather forecasters say a "front" is on the way, then expect the weather to become wet and windy. A warm front is where a mass of warm moist air is pushed up over a mass of colder, drier air creating clouds and rain. Fronts move along with areas of low pressure, and the winds blow stronger as they pass by.

Wispy warning
When you see wisps of feathery cirrus clouds in the sky, you can be sure a warm front is on the way.

Clouding over
After a while, the sky gets hazy and the clouds thicken. Fluffy altocumulus clouds appear, looking like streaks of cotton balls. The wind grows stronger, making the sea very choppy.

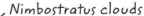
Nimbostratus clouds

Wet and windy
Soon the sky is dark with thick nimbostratus clouds.
It begins to rain steadily and continues to rain for
several hours. If it is cold enough, it may even snow.

Red line
On weather maps, a warm front is a line
with red bumps on it. The bumps point
the same way as the wind blows.

A cold front

Fronts usually come in pairs. Often there is only a brief gap between one front passing and the next arriving. The first is a "warm" front because it brings warmer air. The second is a "cold" front, and brings colder air and sometimes even stormier weather than the warm front.

Stratocumulus clouds bring occasional drizzle.

On the move
On a weather map, a cold front is a line with blue spikes. The spikes show which way the cold air is moving.

Brief relief
As the warm front moves away, the rain (or snow) stops and it gets warmer. Near the coast it stays cloudy, and there may be drizzling rain.

In summer, inland, the Sun comes out and it can get hot after the warm front has moved away.

Storm overhead

You know the cold front is on its way when the wind becomes stronger, giving gusts that rattle windows. The sky may fill with huge dark thunderclouds that lash the countryside with rain or even hailstones.

The sea is very rough.

> More rain may fall in the few minutes a cold front passes than all the hours of a warm front!

It's all over

The worst of the storm is soon over. It feels colder as the clouds clear, leaving a blue sky with fluffy cumulus clouds. However, there may still be more violent showers to come.

The sea is calmer.

Thunder and lightning

Hot, sticky summer days often end in violent thunderstorms. Dark, towering thunderclouds send forks of lightning flashing across the sky, and booming thunderclaps fill the air. The electricity from just one bolt of lightning could light a small town for a whole year!

Flash and crack

Inside a storm cloud, violent winds swirl snow, hailstones, and rain up and down. Electricity builds up in the cloud and escapes as a flash of lightning.

Lightning flash between the bottom of the thundercloud and the ground

Lightning and thunder happen at the same time, but you see the lightning first because light moves faster than sound. Thunder is the sound of air bursting as it is heated rapidly by lightning.

Strike

Lightning always takes the quickest path to the ground. So tall trees and buildings are most likely to be struck. The world's tallest buildings are struck by lightning hundreds of times each year.

Each fork of lightning is many lightning flashes running rapidly up and down the same path.

You can figure out how far away a storm is by counting the seconds between a flash of lightning and a thunderclap. For every three seconds you count, the storm is half a mile (1 km) away.

Holy thunder

Some Native Americans believed that the sacred thunderbird made thunder by beating its enormous wings, and that lightning flashed from its beak.

Colors in the sky

The sky isn't always blue, even when it's clear. Near sunset it can be purple or even red. This is because sunlight is made up of the seven colors of the rainbow, all mixed up together. As sunlight bounces in different ways off dust and other particles in the air, different colors appear.

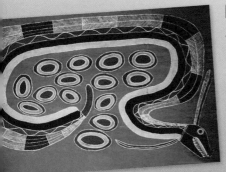

Rainbow Snake
Australian Aboriginals worship a spirit known as the Rainbow Snake. He lives in water and is the great creator who has made the features of the Earth. He can appear as a rainbow.

Rainbows are curved because of the way light hits the round raindrops.

Curving colors
When sunlight passes through raindrops in the air, the light splits into seven colors—red, orange, yellow, green, blue, indigo, and violet. Many raindrops help to create the pattern.

Ring around the Sun

When the Sun shines through thin icy cloud, a colored halo may appear. This is caused by ice crystals in the cloud splitting sunlight into the seven colors, just as raindrops do. Never look directly at the Sun, as it will damage your eyes!

MAKE A RAINBOW

You can make your own rainbow with just a glass of water and bright sunlight. Stand the glass on white paper, facing the Sun. The sunlight will shine through the glass and split into the seven colors.

You always see the colors in a rainbow in the same order, from red through to violet.

Sometimes there is a second, outer bow, and its colors are always the other way around.

To see a rainbow, the Sun must always be behind you.

Changing weather

The world's weather has changed many times. About 10,000 years ago, great sheets of ice covered a third of the Earth. That was the last Ice Age. Today we live in a much warmer climate. Many scientists think we have harmed the atmosphere so much that the world is getting even warmer.

Prehistoric weather

Millions of years ago, when dinosaurs roamed the land, much of Europe and North America was covered in forests. The climate was hotter and more humid than it is today.

Sun trap

Only a small portion of the Sun's heat reaches the Earth. But the Earth stays warm because gases, such as carbon dioxide, trap the heat—just like the glass in a greenhouse. Carbon dioxide is a greenhouse gas that is made when we burn wood, coal, or oil. If we produce too much, the Earth may get too warm.

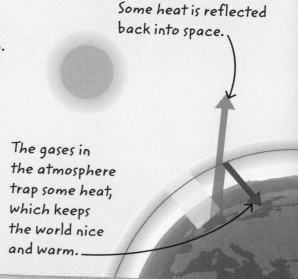

Some heat is reflected back into space.

The gases in the atmosphere trap some heat, which keeps the world nice and warm.

A big umbrella

When volcanoes erupt, they throw large amounts of dust and smoke high into the atmosphere. This cuts off sunlight, shading the ground like a big umbrella. This can make temperatures drop all over the world for a year or more.

Save the trees

Trees take in carbon dioxide and release oxygen and moisture, which is turned to rain. Cutting down the trees stops them doing this, and burning them releases all the carbon dioxide they soaked up as they grew, helping to raise the Earth's temperature.

Tropical rain forests are vital in removing excess carbon dioxide from the air. But in the Amazon region, an area of rain forest the size of Britain is cut down ever year for farming.

Pollution

You may find it hard to believe, but many things people do every day create pollution. Too much pollution can cause changes in the weather. It may get too hot in some places, and cause floods or drought in others. Cutting down on pollution now means a cleaner world tomorrow!

Pollution problems

Smoke and gases from factories pollute the air and may form smog. This is a mixture of smoke and fog, which can make people sick. Car exhausts may give off poisonous gases that not only affect our lungs but can also block out the sunlight.

Acid rain

Power plants that burn coal or oil to generate electricity release waste gases into the air. The gases drift on the wind until raindrops dissolve them, making "acid rain." This eats away at buildings and kills trees, plants, and life in rivers and lakes.

Acid rain, carried by wind, can destroy pine forests thousands of miles away.

TEST FOR ACID RAIN

Here is an experiment you can use to test for acid in rainwater. You will need two finely chopped red cabbage leaves, distilled water (from a pharmacy), rainwater, a bowl, two glass jars, a measuring cup, and a sieve.

1. Put the leaves into the bowl. Have an adult pour hot distilled water over them. Then let them stand for an hour.

2. Strain the cabbage juice into a measuring cup. The liquid should be a dark purple color.

3. Pour 1 fl oz (20 ml) of distilled water into one jar, and 1 fl oz (20 ml) of rainwater, collected from your yard, into the other.

4. Add the same amount of cabbage juice to each jar. The water will change color. Compare the color of the distilled water (this stays the same) and the rainwater. If the rainwater turns red, it is acidic.

Rainwater

Distilled water

The stronger the acid, the redder the water gets.

The Earth's blanket

The ozone layer of our atmosphere protects us from the Sun's harmful ultraviolet rays. However, some chemicals can destroy it. As a result, holes have appeared in the ozone layer, allowing more of the harmful rays to reach the Earth's surface and damage many living things.

The blue areas in this satellite photograph show the hole in the ozone layer over the Antarctic.

53

Weather lore

Today, weather forecasters use satellites and radar to tell us what the weather holds. Before this, people used to look for clues in nature to predict the weather. They didn't just look at the skies—they also watched how animals and plants acted. Some of the signs are reliable, but others aren't foolproof!

Groundhog forecast
In the United States, people say that if you can see a groundhog's shadow at noon on February 2, there will be six more weeks of winter. Fortunately, the groundhog isn't always right!

Red sky at night
People used to say a red sunrise meant bad weather to come, and that a red sunset meant good weather to come. Try to watch the sky at sunrise and sunset to see if this saying is always correct.

Pinecones are traditionally used to forecast the weather. Put a pinecone outdoors and watch what happens. It will open out in very dry weather and close up when it is damp.

The pinecone's scales open in dry weather.

Scales are tightly shut in wet weather.

Flower power

When you want to know what the weather will be like, look for the magic carpet flower. It grows in the wild in South Africa and is a popular garden plant elsewhere. The petals stay wide open in clear weather, but they close up when the sky grows dark.

Frog-cast

One way to tell if it's going to rain soon is to look out for frogs. They love to come out when it's damp. Since the air becomes humid before it rains, you may see more frogs around and you will know to expect rain.

Weather forecasting

To figure out what weather is on its way, forecasters take measurements from weather stations all over the world. They also study information gathered by satellites in space. The information is entered into powerful computers that work out how it might affect the atmosphere. The results are then used to forecast how the weather is going to change.

Solar panels

Weather satellite
Satellites in space are controlled by teams of people on Earth, but they can perform many tasks automatically.

WEATHER SYMBOLS

Every type of weather has a special symbol. Keep track of the weather for a week, and see how many different symbols you use.

Sunny

Sunny intervals

Cloudy

Light rain

Heavy rain

Thundery showers

Hail showers

Heavy snow

Weather map

Information about the weather is often shown on maps. Places where the atmospheric pressure is the same are joined by lines called isobars. The isobars form rings around zones of low pressure and high pressure.

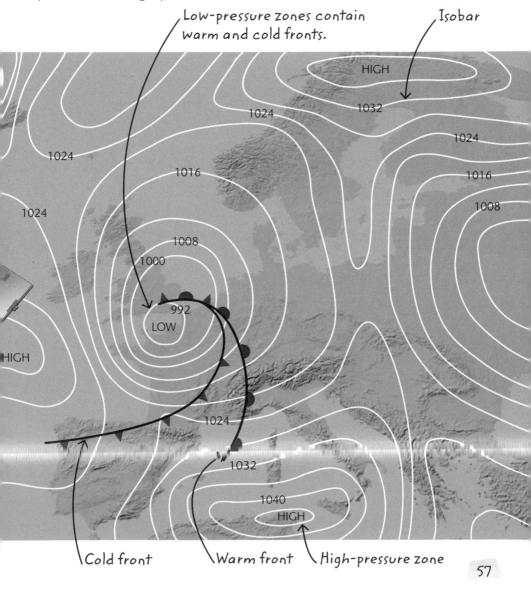

Low-pressure zones contain warm and cold fronts.

Isobar

HIGH

1024

1032

1024

1024

1016

1024

1016

1008

1008

1000

992

LOW

HIGH

1024

1032

1040

HIGH

Cold front

Warm front

High-pressure zone

The day

During the course of each day there are changes in the weather. On days with good weather, you can almost tell the time by the way the weather changes through the day— from the cool chill of dawn through the heat of the afternoon to the clear, calm evening.

Sun rise

Dawn is usually chilly, as the ground loses heat steadily all night. It is often misty, too, for the cool of the night makes water condense in the air.

Noon

As the Sun climbs in the sky, morning mists fade away and it gets warmer. By noon, a few fluffy cumulus clouds appear, made by rising warm, moist air.

Toward sunset

As the Sun drops lower toward sunset, its power to stir up the air gets less and less. So the end of the day is often calm and clear, with barely a cloud in the sky.

Midafternoon

Midafternoon is the warmest time of the day. Often, though, the morning's fluffy cumulus clouds can build up and up until they interrupt the afternoon with brief but heavy showers of rain, or even thunderstorms.

Night

Once the Sun has dropped below the horizon it gets steadily colder—especially if there are no clouds to keep the heat in.

Index

R

rain 17, 18–19, 20–21, 56
rain gauge 21
raindrops 20
rainbows 48–49
rain forests 51
rime frost 25

S

satellites 9, 56
seasons 10–11
showers 19, 45, 56, 59
smog 52
snow 20, 26–27, 46
solar power 36
spring 10
storms 45, 46
stratocumulus clouds 15, 44
stratosphere 9
stratus clouds 13, 14
summer 11
Sun 10–11, 14, 17, 24, 36–37, 38, 40, 44, 50, 52, 58–59
sunset 48, 54, 59

TV

temperature 36, 30–31
thermometers 36
thermosphere 9
thunderstorms 15, 34, 45, 46–47, 59
tornadoes 15, 34–35
tropical cyclones 32
troposphere 9
twisters 34–35
typhoons 32

volcanoes 51

W

warm fronts 42–43, 44, 57
water 8
water cycle 17
water vapor 16–17, 18, 20, 23, 37
waterspouts 35
weather maps 43, 44, 57
wind 9, 28–29
wind power 29
winter 10, 11, 24–25, 26–27

Acknowledgments

Dorling Kindersley would like to thank:

Carl Gombrich, Gin von Noorden, and Kate Raworth for editorial assistance and research.
Sharon Grant and Faith Nelson for design assistance.
Ron Lobeck for help with writing text.
Hilary Bird for the index.
Jim Sharp for help with authenticating text.